PLANETS

MARS

ABDO
Publishing Company

A Buddy Book by Fran Howard

VISIT US AT

www.abdopublishing.com

Published by ABDO Publishing Company, 8000 West 78th Street, Edina, Minnesota 55439.

Printed in the United States.

Editor: Sarah Tieck
Contributing Editor: Michael P. Goecke
Graphic Design: Maria Hosley
Cover Image: NASA and The Hubble Heritage Team (STSci/AURA).
Interior Images: Getty Images (page 23); Library of Congress (page 23); Lushpix (page 9, 10–11); NASA (page 29); NASA: Ames Research Center (page 5), Goddard Space Flight Center Scientific Visualization Studio (page 4, 13), Glen Research Center (page 29), Jet Propulsion Laboratory (page 6–7, 12, 26, 27, 28, 30), JPL / Malin Space Science Systems (page 17), Kennedy Space Center (page 26), Langley Research Center (page 25); Photos.com (page 15, 21).

Library of Congress Cataloging-in-Publication Data

Howard, Fran, 1953-
  Mars / Fran Howard.
     p. cm. -- (The planets)
  Includes index.
  ISBN 978-1-59928-826-0
  1. Mars (Planet)--Juvenile literature. I. Title.

  QB641.H688 2008
  523.43--dc22

                        2007014756

Table Of Contents

The Planet Mars

Mars is a planet. A planet is a large body in space.

Planets travel around stars. The path a planet travels is its orbit. When a planet circles a star, it is orbiting the star.

The sun is a star. Mars orbits the sun. The sun's gravity holds Mars in place as it circles.

Earth is a planet too. Mars is about half the size of Earth.

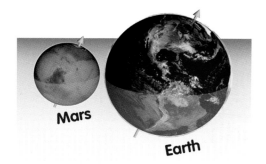

Mars

Earth

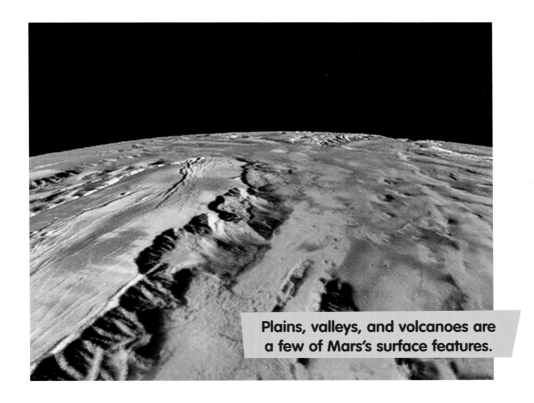

Plains, valleys, and volcanoes are a few of Mars's surface features.

Mars orbits the sun in about 687 Earth days. That means a year on Mars is about twice as long as a year on Earth.

Our Solar System

OUTER PLANETS

Neptune
Uranus
Saturn
Jupiter

Mars's Orbit

Mars is one of eight planets that orbit our sun. The planets orbiting the sun make up our solar system.

The other planets in our solar system are Mercury, Venus, Earth, Jupiter, Saturn, Uranus, and Neptune.

Mars is about 142 million miles (229 million km) from the sun. It is the fourth-closest planet to the sun.

SUN

Mars

Earth

Venus

Mercury

INNER PLANETS

The Red Planet

Mars is very visible in Earth's sky. Only the sun, Earth's moon, and Venus are brighter. Sometimes, Mars can even be seen from Earth without a telescope.

Mars is called "The Red Planet." This name comes from the red rocks and dust that cover the planet's surface.

The rocks and dust on Mars's surface contain iron. Iron's color makes the planet look red.

A Dramatic Landscape

Mars has some of the deepest valleys in the solar system. The southern part of the planet is covered with large basins. These are called impact craters. They were made when large objects hit the planet.

Mars also has some of the solar system's tallest volcanoes. The largest is called Olympus Mons. It towers about 15 miles (24 km) above the surface of Mars. Some say it is the highest mountain in the solar system!

A Mars rover saw this view of the planet's surface in 2005.

11

The sky on Mars is not blue like on Earth. It is an orange brown color.

Two moons orbit Mars. These moons are shaped like potatoes. The gravity of Mars captured these moons.

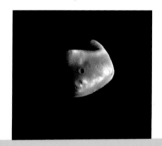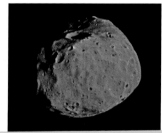

Mars has two rocky moons, Deimos *(left)* and Phobos *(right)*.

Some scientists think water once flowed on Mars. But today, dust storms and ice cover the planet's surface.

Nothing is known to live on Mars. Still, some scientists think tiny life-forms could live there.

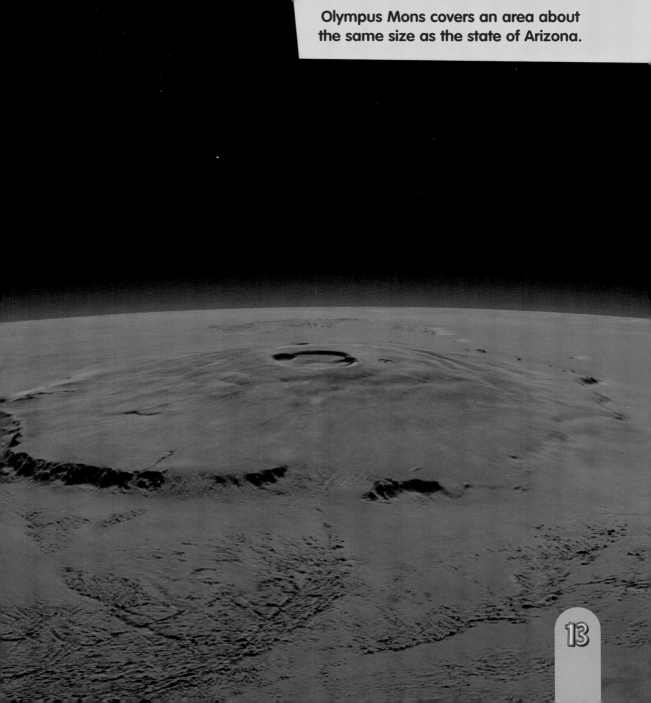

Olympus Mons covers an area about the same size as the state of Arizona.

13

What Is It Like There?

Layers of gases surround each planet in our solar system. These layers form each planet's atmosphere. The atmosphere on Mars is made mostly of carbon dioxide. It is dusty there.

Planets spin on an axis. This spinning creates night and day. Mars makes one complete spin in slightly more than 24 hours.

A day on Mars is about the same length as a day on Earth.

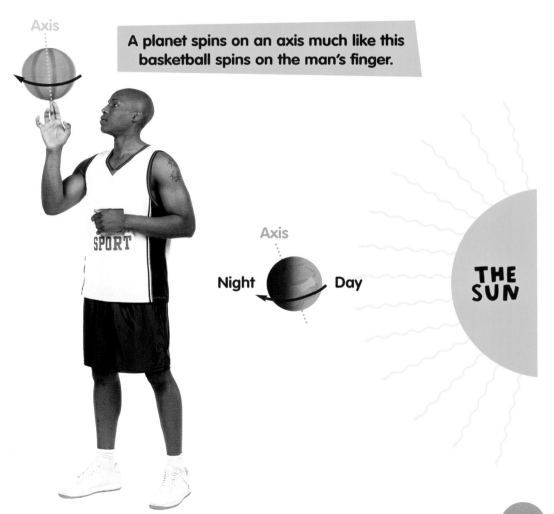

Axis

A planet spins on an axis much like this basketball spins on the man's finger.

SPORT

Axis

Night

Day

THE SUN

Mars is a very cold planet. Its temperatures fall to about -200 degrees Fahrenheit (-130°C) in winter. Temperatures can reach 80 degrees Fahrenheit (27°C) in summer.

Mars gets so cold in winter that part of the carbon dioxide in its atmosphere turns into dry ice. In summer, the dry ice turns back into a gas.

This change causes strong winds. These winds create big dust storms. Some of the dust storms cover the entire planet. These storms are similar to hurricanes on Earth.

Scientists think seasonal changes cause the color
differences between Saturn's top and bottom halves.

A Gas Giant

Scientists think Saturn may have a rocky core. But, it does not have a surface to stand on.

This is because Saturn is a gas giant. Gas giants are mostly made of gas. Jupiter, Uranus, and Neptune are also gas giants.

The center of Saturn is very hot. Its temperature can reach 21,092 degrees Fahrenheit (11,700°C)! Above the center is a liquid layer, followed by the gas layer. Above this, the atmosphere forms the outer layer.

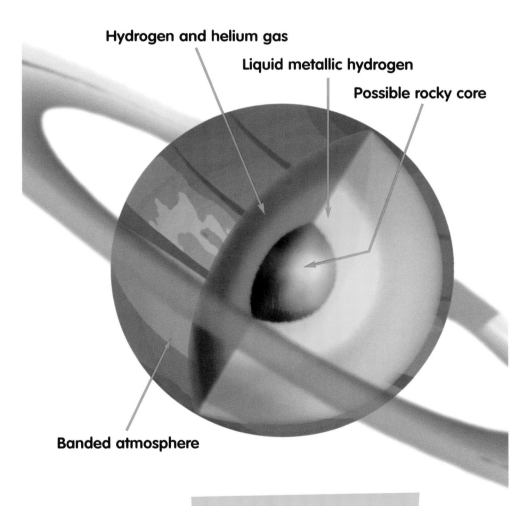

Hydrogen and helium gas

Liquid metallic hydrogen

Possible rocky core

Banded atmosphere

Gas giants have layers, but
no surfaces to stand on.

Discovering Saturn

No one knows who discovered Saturn. But, it is visible in Earth's night sky. So, people on Earth have known about it since early times.

The Romans named Saturn after their god of farming.

On a clear night, it is possible to see
Saturn without using a telescope.

In 1659, Christiaan Huygens thought Saturn had one big ring circling it.

In 1675, Jean-Dominique Cassini discovered that Saturn's ring was actually many small rings.

Almost 200 years later, James Clerk Maxwell also studied Saturn's rings. He determined that they are made of small objects.

Galileo was the first person to see Saturn's rings.
He saw them through a telescope in 1610.

Missions To Saturn

In 1979, *Pioneer 11* became the first spacecraft to fly by Saturn. It studied Saturn's rings. It also measured the temperature of the moon Titan.

In 1980, *Voyager 1* took images of Saturn, its rings, and its moons. *Voyager 1* also flew close to Titan. It discovered that clouds cover this moon.

One year later, *Voyager 2* took more images of Saturn and its rings.

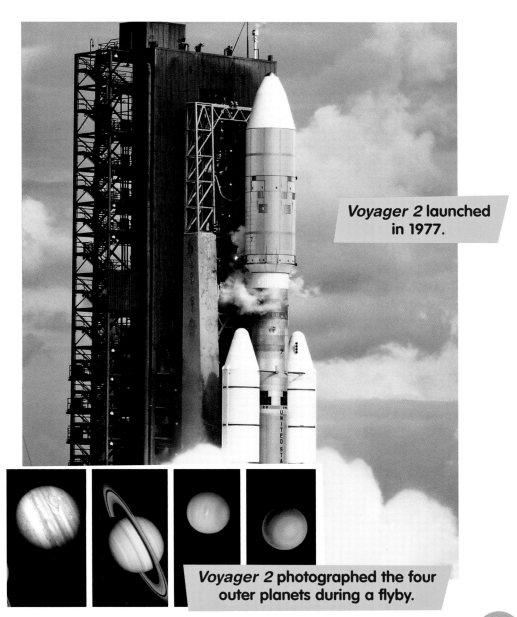

Voyager 2 launched in 1977.

Voyager 2 photographed the four outer planets during a flyby.

Scientists have learned a lot about Saturn, its rings, and its moons from the *Cassini-Huygens* mission. The mission's spacecraft launched in 1997. In 2004, it reached Saturn.

The *Cassini-Huygens* spacecraft sent a probe to Titan on December 25, 2004. The probe found liquid methane and evidence of precipitation. It also discovered that some of Titan's rocks are actually made of frozen water.

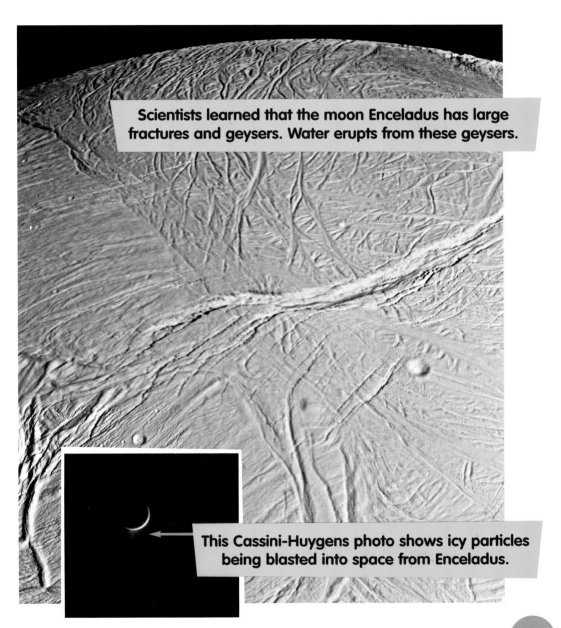

Scientists learned that the moon Enceladus has large fractures and geysers. Water erupts from these geysers.

This Cassini-Huygens photo shows icy particles being blasted into space from Enceladus.

Fact Trek

The symbol for Saturn is a sickle. Long ago, farmers used sickles to harvest grain.

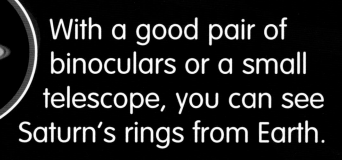

With a good pair of binoculars or a small telescope, you can see Saturn's rings from Earth.

Saturn is a very light planet. If it were placed in water, Saturn would float.

Every 14 years, Saturn's rings seem to disappear. This happens when the rings face Earth edge on.

Saturn's major rings are only 330 feet (100 m) thick.

Voyage To Tomorrow

People are continuing to explore space. They want to learn more about Saturn.

The *Cassini-Huygens* spacecraft began orbiting Saturn on July 1, 2004. By the end of its mission in 2008, it orbited Saturn 74 times.

The Cassini-Huygens spacecraft flew by Venus, Earth, and Jupiter before reaching Saturn.

Important Words

atmosphere   the layer of gases that surrounds a planet.

axis   an imaginary line through a planet. Planets spin around this line.

gravity   the force that draws things toward a planet and prevents them from floating away. Stars use this force to keep planets in their orbit.

methane   an odorless, colorless gas that burns easily. Sometimes it is used for fuel.

mission   the sending of spacecraft to perform specific jobs.

precipitation   rain, snow, or other moisture that falls from the sky.

probe   a spacecraft that attempts to gather information.

spacecraft   a vehicle that travels in space.

Web Sites

To learn more about **Saturn**, visit ABDO Publishing Company on the World Wide Web. Web sites about **Saturn** are featured on our Book Links page. These links are routinely monitored and updated to provide the most current information available.

www.abdopublishing.com

31

INDEX